Needle Felting Winter

By
Rachel Austin

This book is dedicated to Steph and Sophie xx

Deep in an enchanted forest, friendly little gnomes called 'The Foresters' dwell within a toadstool village. They love the wintertime, and they invite the forest creatures, great and small, to share homemade walnut cake and warming pine needle tea.

Contents

Introduction

My name is Rachel Austin. I'm a full time artist/crafter at 'The Wishing Shed' and mother of two beautiful girls. I love needing felting and creating lifelike animals and various whimsical figures. Along my crafting journey, I've dabbled in a few different mediums, such as clay and painting, but I always seem to come back to needle felting. There is just something so charming about pieces created with wool. And now, as this craft is growing more and more in popularity, I want to share a range of my designs and felting ideas. So, I've created this book full of projects that cater to both beginners and more advanced needle felters.

Although the projects in this book have a winter theme, the techniques and ideas can be applied to many other felted works.

Whether you're a beginner or advanced needle felter, I hope you enjoy these projects, and I hope they give you a little inspiration.

Love,

Rachel

xx

Many of you have probably heard about 'Needle Felting' and know what it is. However, if you are a beginner, here is a brief explanation.

Needle felting is basically the process of sculpting with wool fibre. By stabbing unspun wool fibre with special barbed felting needles, you can create unique 2D and 3D works of art, cute gifts, toys, and more. The more you stab the wool with the needles, the more the fibres agitate and firm together. There really are no limitations to the shapes you can make. Just let your imagination go wild!

I find wool is very forgiving, and you do not have to be an artist to create wonderful felted pieces. However, like any craft, it does take a bit of practice. Sometimes I like my pieces to be soft and fluffy, so I don't felt too much, but other times, if I want more density and definition, I spend a longer time felting for a firmer, more detailed result.

Materials & Tools

The materials I've listed here are what I've used for the projects in this book. Most of them are inexpensive, and you may find that you already have them lying about your house.

Tools:

1) Felting Needles—36-star (medium gauge) and 38-star (fine gauge.) If you are a beginner in felting, I recommend using leather 'finger guards', as felting needles are extremely sharp. On that note, I personally do not recommend needle felting for children under the age of twelve. Older children should be supervised at all times by an adult.

2) Pink clover felting pen, or other 'multi-needle tool'. A 'pen handle' that holds three or more needles at once is a great investment, as it felts wool on a larger scale quicker and more efficiently.

3) Needle felting surface. (I always use foam sponges.)

4) Needle felting awl tool. This tool has a sharp, long metal point, perfect for making 'eye sockets' and holes in felted dolls and toys. I use my felting needle, but if you're making lots of dolls, this tool comes in handy.

5) Wire — 24 gauge

6) Pipe cleaners

7) Fabric transfer pen

8) Coloured marker pens. I love the Copic brand.

9) Small 'glass bead eyes'

10) Small 'stem-bead eyes'

11) Sharp scissors

12) Small, 'pre-felted' balls in flesh colour (either 1 cm or 1.5 cm.)

13) Wire cutters

14) Pliers

15) Needle and thread

16) Ruler or tape measure

17) Fabric glue (or a good-quality PVA glue)

18) Hot glue gun

19) Paint brush

20) Cardboard tubes

21) Scraps of lace, ribbons, or fabric

22) Embroidery thread and needle

23) Glitter glue (not essential)

24) 3D fabric paints (not essential)

25) Small, coloured beads, and 4–5 mm sequins

26) Wooden cocktail sticks

Wool

If you mainly want to create larger 3D needle-felted projects, then a good carded core wool with a higher micron count is a must-have. Carded 'Dorset Horn' or 'Corriedale' also work reasonably well as a core wool.

When I started out needle felting, I spent so much money on wool I couldn't use in the end because it didn't produce the detail that I was trying so hard to create. Carded wool (sometimes known as 'batts') with a higher micron count of over 23, leaves less 'stabbing holes' behind from the felting needles. The carded wool I tend to use nowadays is carded 'New Zealand', or a 'Bergschaf' blend. For Waldorf-style doll hair, I often use 'Corriedale tops'. It's more durable than 'merino tops' and works well for creating all different hairstyles.

Another must-have is merino pre-felt. In my opinion, 'merino tops' do not always suit 3D pieces, but the pre-felt is great for making so many things, and I've shown few examples in projects throughout this book. I also like to use natural wool pre-felt, such as 'Shetland', for some of my 3D pieces.

You can find some of the wool and wonderful pre-felt in my online Etsy shop, along with other felting kits and accessories. I also have demonstration tutorials on my YouTube channel, **'The Wishing Shed'**.

Cream Carded Core Wool.
(27 Micron.) Perfect for 3D sculptures.

Carded New Zealand Wool.
(Un-dyed/Natural Shades)

Curly Locks.
(I love Wensleydale and Blue Faced Leicester)

Wool 'Tops'
(Merino and Corriedale 'tops' pictured right.)

'Tops' are wools that have been combed as opposed to carded, therefore, they're harder to needle felt. I do find, however, that merino tops create beautiful effects in 2D-felted works and pictures.

Corriedale tops, at first glance, look similar to merino tops, but it has a higher micron, meaning it's more durable and needle felts easier.

Wool 'pre-felt'
Great for both Nuno felting & 2D & 3D Projects.

1mm Wool Felt. Much more durable than acrylic felt and as it's made of wool, it adheres to felting well.

Mohair Yarn. Great for dolls hair or adding fur to fuzzy animals. Knitting wool can also be used for dolls hair. I often brush knitting wool to separate it using a carding brush or a dog hair brush.

Sparkly Angelina fibre. This material adds a little magic to your wool pieces and can be found in a variety of colours.

Now that we've covered the basics, let's begin needle felting needle felting 'Winter'.

The Swan

You Will Need:

Cotton pipe cleaners; cream or white 'pre-felt' (preferably Shetland wool); carded New Zealand wool in white and black; 1 mm thick, white wool felt; small, 1 to 2 mm flat-back gems/crystals; PVA or fabric glue; 38- and 36-gauge felting needles; and a felting surface.
Optional: Silver embroidery thread and needle or silver fabric paint.

Head and Neck

Begin by cutting your chenille/cotton pipe cleaner to around 4 inches in length. Dip the tip of one end into some fabric or PVA glue and smooth it around with your fingers to form a pointed beak. Alternatively, if you want to use non-cotton pipe cleaners, you can wrap orange-coloured wool around the tip and then smooth it with the glue. You may want to use a white cotton pipe cleaner instead of the orange one (because the neck of the swan is thin, a little orange may show through if not wrapped tightly enough). If using a white, cotton pipe cleaner, simply colour the beak in with an orange marker pen once dry.

Next, wrap a thin strip of white carded wool all the way down the pipe cleaner, excluding the beak. Carefully needle felt into place and add a little more wool around the top to build up the head. Now vigorously roll the covered pipe cleaner back and forth between the palms of your hands to even out and smooth the fibres.

The Body

Take a sheet of pre-felt (I used Shetland A4 size) and cut a diagonal strip, starting at around 2 inches down the longest side and finishing at a point. Lay the bottom end of the neck pipe cleaner onto the thickest end of the pre-felt strip, and roll it up tightly. You should be left with a nice oval shape. Needle felt all over to secure the felt in place.

Wrap thin strips of white carded wool around your swan's body and up onto the bottom section of the neck, then needle felt into place.

Bend the neck into an 'S' shape with your fingers, and pinch and shape the tail end into a point. Next, needle felt black carded wool across the top of the beak area, tapering it thinner on the sides of the head where the eyes are going to go.

Adding stem eyes can be tricky on this scale, so I used tiny 2 mm black crystal gems for swan eyes and glued them in place with fabric glue.

TIP: Tweezers come in handy for this part.

The Wings

Trace the wing template onto paper, cut out, and pin onto wool felt, then cut out two felt wings.

Wing

Look from above when positioning the wings onto the sides of your swan's body. One at a time, attach the wings into place by needle felting white carded wool over the bottom areas of each wing, through, and into the body.

Finally, if desired, add detail to the wings by sewing silver lines with embroidery thread, or draw on lines with silver fabric paint.

I couldn't decide which owl design to add, so I thought I would show you how to make both!

Snowy Owl

You Will Need:

Cream or white core wool; white, black, and grey carded New Zealand wool; one wooden cocktail stick; black embroidery thread; gold sequins; black marker pen; fabric glue, 38- and 36-gauge felting needles; and a felting surface.

Begin by taking a strip of core wool (around 1 inch thick by 4 inches long), and roll it up as tightly as you can. Needle felt it all over and shape into a figure eight. Felt the base flat, then felt a little extra core wool at the back for a tail, and use your fingers to help shape it into a point.
(See diagram of the side view.)

Wrap a thin, even layer of white carded wool over your owl's body and head, needle felting it all over into place. Once fully covered, hold the body upright, and vigorously rub it back and forth on a hard surface, such as a tabletop.
This will help to further flatten the base so your owl stands up nicely. Next, take a small amount of dark-grey wool and roll it between your fingers, teasing and pulling it until it's threadlike. Use your felting needle to 'draw' on grey detail around the front edges of your owl. Now take small bits of black carded wool and needle felt two circles where your owl's eyes are going to go. If you are using sequin eyes, the black circles need to be slightly larger than the sequins. The black wool will help the sequins really stand out. Once the sequin eyes are glued in place, use a black marker to colour a small dot over the pupil area to enlarge it. Next, use thin strands of black wool to draw little 'V' shapes for feathers on the chest area, or embroider them on with black embroidery thread.

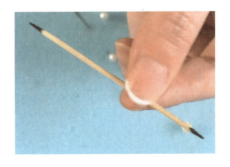

Last, use your felting needle or an awl to make a hole where the beak is going to go, then colour in the tip of the cocktail stick with a black marker and carefully cut a beak using scissors or wire cutters. Use a dab of fabric glue to secure the beak into place.

Brown Owl

You Will Need:

Brown carded Corriedale wool or Manx Langton, black carded wool or black merino pre-felt for the beak, grey pre-felt, white/cream merino pre-felt, black 2mm stem bead eyes, 38* 36* felting needles, felting surface.

NOTE: As with this brown owl, you don't always have to use core wool for a project, especially if they are small.

   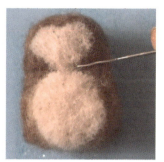

Roll up your brown carded wool (around 1 inch thick by 5 inches long) as tightly as you can and needle felt all over for around 5 minutes to shape it into a 'figure 8' shape. Felt the base flat and shape a tail as you did for the snowy owl. Next, cut out a small circle of the cream pre-felt and needle felt it onto your owls tummy. Then cut out a small heart shape and needle felt it onto the face.

Use your fingers to pull and shape the wool into two little ears at the back of the head. You may need to add a little more wool for the ears, or you can take a strong sewing needle, insert it into the wool area where you want the ears to be, and gently 'pull' the needle up to lift and shape the ears.

Next measure out two equal amounts of wool to make two little 'leaf shape' wings and one at a time needle felt them onto the sides of your owl. If needed felt a little spare brown wool over the join area onto the body for extra hold. Needle felt the tips of the wings around the body so that they meet on the back. Use a thin thread like strip of brown carded wool to 'draw' on the 'V' feather detail onto your owls tummy.

Using the line of your needle, work out an even position for the eyes, and then carefully push your needle (or felting awl) right through to make the eye 'sockets'. Add fabric glue to the stem of your stem-back eyes, and push each one into place. It helps the stem eyes go into the wool if you twist them as you push.

Cut a small corner off black pre-felt, and roll it between your fingers to make a little beak. Carefully needle felt it onto your owl, just below the eyes.

For the feet, cut off a corner of grey pre-felt, and cut and round off the edges. Roll the front section back, and needle felt to secure. Then needle felt a line down the middle to create the look of two feet.

Needle felt or glue the feet onto the base of your owl.

I just love making these little fairies, and the great thing is, no wire armature is needed.

Snow Fairies

You Will Need:

Merino pre-felt in flesh; small flesh-coloured felted balls 1 to 1.5 cm; white Corriedale tops for the hair (or wool yarn); white, 1 mm thick wool felt; feathers for the wings (or tulle fabric) scraps of lace/fabric/ribbon; fabric glue or hot glue gun; 38- and 36-gauge felting needles; and a felting surface.

Arms and Legs

Cut a thin strip of flesh-coloured pre-felt (approximately 5 inches long by 6 mm thick), then cut it in half so you have two equal, smaller lengths. One at a time, needle felt the strips, and vigorously roll each end between your fingers. Do not felt the middle section.

Add a few drops of washing-up liquid mixed with water, and use the mixture to smooth and round each end of the strips for the hands and feet.

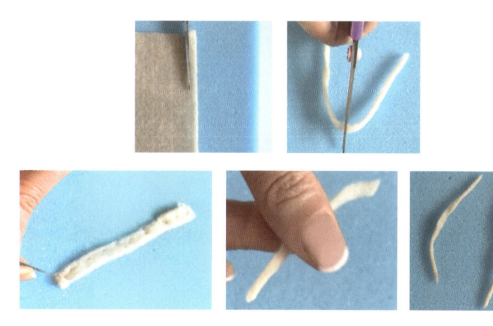

Body

Cut a triangle shape on the fold of the pre-felt. *(See template.)*

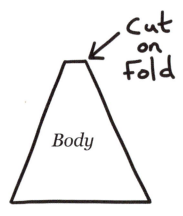

Needle felt around the neck area, and roll between your fingers to smooth.

Sandwich the middle section of the arms and legs between the triangle body pieces, and needle felt them into place on the bottom triangle section. Needle felt a little more rolled up pre-felt or core wool to fatten up the body, then fold the top triangle piece down and needle felt it into place.

Hairstyle #1

For the head, I used flesh-coloured, 1.5 cm 'pre-felted' balls.
There are various ways of making the hair. I like to use Corriedale tops.
I also like to use fuzzy mohair yarn, or just good old knitting wool. Curly wool locks, such as Bluefaced Leicester or Wensleydale, also make nice hair for felted dolls.

Take a strip of Corriedale tops and fold it in half. Lay the fold on top of your fairy's head so the fold creates the 'fringe', and let the rest go straight down the back of the head. Lay another strip of unfolded Corriedale sideways on top of the head, and needle felt a line or parting firmly down the middle top section of the head. This should 'root' the hair into place. Once in place, smooth and shape the hair down around the head with your fingers.

Hairstyle #2

Wrap mohair yarn around your finer to form a sort of 'doughnut of wool'. Use fabric glue or a hot glue gun to attach to the felted ball head in the 'doughnut' centre. Then make a smaller 'doughnut/bun', and glue it to the back of the existing circle of hair.

Hats

Cut a curved corner off of some wool felt, and sew the two straight edges together using a backstitch or blanket stitch. Turn right way out using a pencil or knitting needle to help shape the pointy tip, and it glue onto the top of your fairy's head.

Dress

Make fairy dresses out of scraps of lace and ribbon.
Wrap them around your fairy and glue or sew into place at the back.

Wings

Draw and cut out a wing shape from some paper, and pin it onto folded tulle or gauze fabric or felt. Cut on the fold so you get a set of even wings. Another option is to simply glue feathers onto the back of your fairy. Glue wings beneath the hair using some fabric glue or a hot glue gun. You can also cut out sets of wings from heat-bonded Angelina fibres, which I explain how use later on.

Snowy Fir Trees

You Will Need:

Green core wool or green carded wool; medium and dark green shades of Corriedale tops; white carded wool; 38- and 36-gauge felting needles; and a felting surface.

Optional: Wooden cotton reel or bottle cork; 6 mm craft pompoms; hot glue gun or fabric glue; brown wool felt.

Needle felt a thin cone shape around 6 to 7 inches high, and with a 2- to 3-inch base. Then cut three equal height sections using sharp scissors. (I generally like to use green carded wool for the core cone, but I have used white for these photos so you can see the process more clearly.)

For the green fir branches, take a strip of dark-green and medium-green Corriedale tops, and blend the two colors together by repeatedly laying the strips on top of each other and pulling them apart. Separate into four equal lengths, and one at a time, lay them across the largest section of the cone going in different directions. Needle felt them into place through the top.

18

Repeat the process of adding the green Corriedale wool strips onto the other two sections of the cut cone pieces. For the tip of the tree, use slightly thinner strips, and needle felt the top point as thinly as you can. Firmly roll the tip of the tree between your fingers to help shape it. Trim off any stray 'fuzz' around the top point of the tree.

Now stack the sections on top of each other. You can needle felt them in place with a thick 'rooting' needle, sew them, or simply use a hot glue gun to secure the sections together.

The trees look nice without a 'stump', but here are a few ideas if you decide you would like to make one.
A) Wooden cotton reel (B) Bottle cork (C) Roll up a small strip of brown pre-felt and needle felt it together to secure.

You can glue any of the above firmly into place with a hot glue gun or fabric glue.

Finally, roll white carded wool between your fingers and wrap it around your tree. Carefully use your fingers or felting needle to pull out a few of the fir branches over it.

You can use Angelina fibres instead of white wool for a glittery effect. Alternatively, glue on miniature pompoms. Why not try swapping green Corriedale for white, and make white trees?

19

Why do we associate the robin with winter? Perhaps, when the landscape is stark and covered in snow, a flash of his colourful red breast is a welcomed sight indeed.

Robin Redbreast

You Will Need:

Core wool, grey/brown; 1 mm wool felt; carded wool in brown, grey, orangey red, dark brown, and white; black pre-felt; 3 mm black beads; 38- and 36-gauge felting needles; a felting surface; and needle and thread. (For the 'non-flying robin', you also need 24-gauge wire; grey merino tops or grey embroidery skein or florist tape for the legs.)

Flying Robin

Begin by needle felting the shapes of the body (using core wool) to roughly fit into the stencil guide provided. Needle felt the body sections together, and add a little extra core wool over the joins until the body pieces are securely in place.

Next, needle felt medium-brown wool onto the top of the robin, going slightly down onto the sides and up over the top of the head. Felt medium-coloured grey wool onto the underside, going slightly up and around onto the sides of the body and front of the face. Felt orangey/red wool over the front of the face, going up just a little onto the top of the head and down onto the chest area. Try leaving some grey showing at the sides of the face.

Insert a strong sewing needle horizontally across the area where the beak is going to go, and 'pull' the wool forwards a little.

Wings and Tail

Use the flying wing template. Cut out the paper stencil, pin onto wool felt, and cut out two wings. I like to use a slightly grey-brown colour for flying wings.

TIP: I find it easier to cut out the 'leaf' shape of the wing first, then cut out the little 'V' shapes to create the look of feathers. Create the flying tail the same way.

One at a time, position the wings onto the side of the robin's body, with the detailed side face up. Use the same medium grey used on the underside of the robin to attach the bottom area of the wings to the body. Felt the wool firmly through the felt wings using a thicker gauge felting needle until they are securely anchored on.

TIP: To get the wings evenly placed, look from above when positioning them.

Attach the tail by felting the grey wool through from the underside and then add the brown wool through the top of the tail until it's held in place.

Work out the position of the first eye and carefully push your felting needle all the way through to get the position for the opposite eye. Next, sew in the eyes following the 'How to Sew Eyes' guide on Page 76. Cut a small corner off black pre-felt, and roll it between your fingers to form a little beak. Dip the tip into PVA/water solution, and smooth again with your fingers. Once dry, needle felt it into place on the middle front of your robin's face, slightly below eye level.

Create the legs following the 'How to Make Wire Legs/Feet' diagram on the Robin Stencil Page. Wrapping thin wire is a bit fiddly. I have used grey embroidery skein here, and a little hot glue to hold in place around the toes. Merino wool tops work quite well for wrapping wire, or try wrapping the wire with black florist tape. If using merino wool to wrap the legs, wrap as tightly and as smoothly as you can, carefully needle felting in place around the wire feet. Dip into a mixture of three parts PVA and one part water, and set aside to dry.

Position the covered legs towards the back of your robin, and needle felt core wool across the middle section to attach them onto the body.

Add the top coat colours the same way you did for The Flying Robin.

Non-Flying Wings and Tail

I like to use brown wool felt for the non-flying robin wings and tail. Cut out the wings, and needle felt brown wool onto the top. Use more brown wool to attach them onto the sides of the body.

Lastly, use a threadlike strip of dark brown wool to add the wing and tail detail.

Non Flying/Flying Robin Stencil - To Scale

Flying Wing
X2
Flying Tail
Felt top sides of head thin
Head
Head-Front
X2
Non Flying Wing
Body
Underside Tail
Beak
Non Flying Tail
Wire length for legs
X2

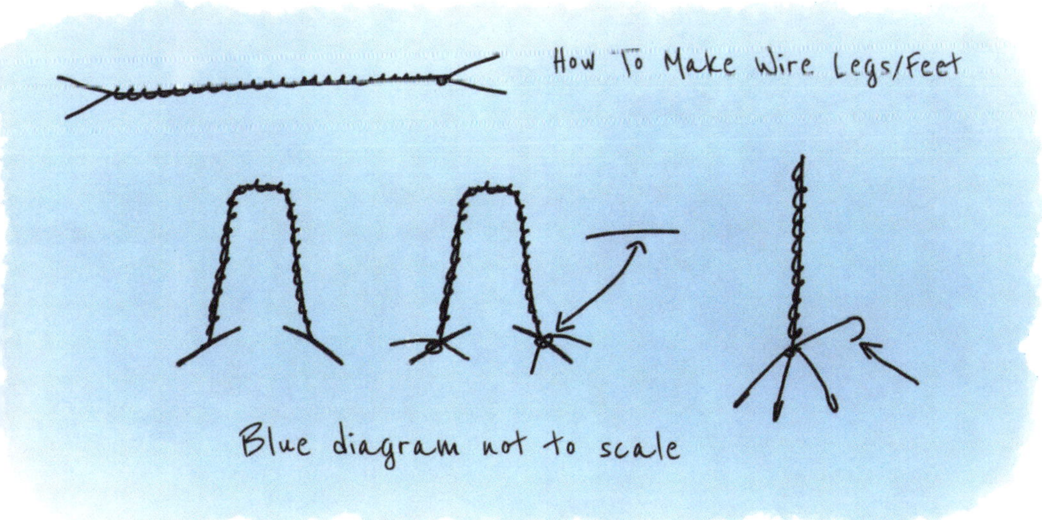

How To Make Wire Legs/Feet
Blue diagram not to scale

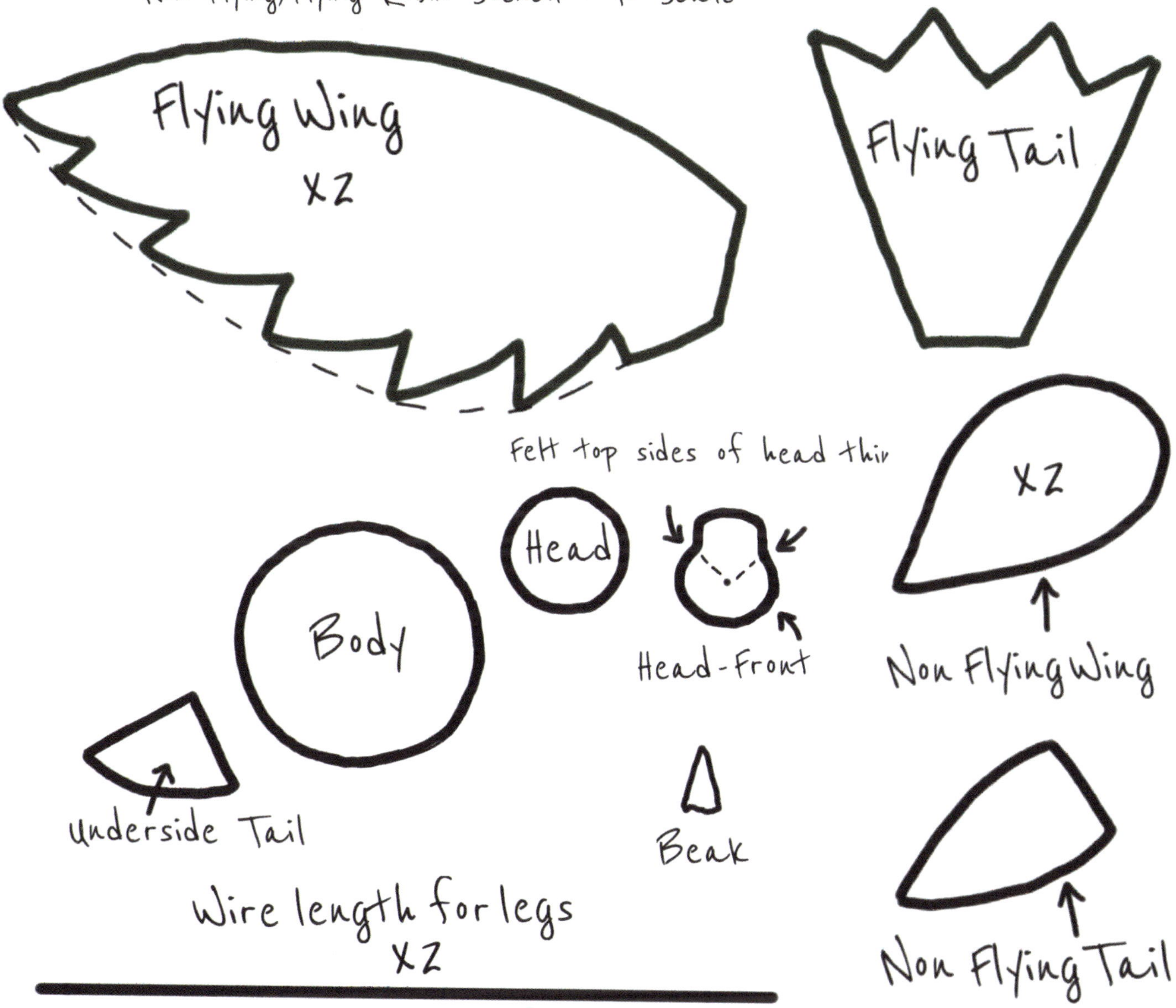

The Hedgehogs

You Will Need:

Carded wool in brown; cream merino pre-felt; 1 mm wool felt in flesh; 2 mm stem-bead eyes; brown fabric paint for the nose; 38- and 36-gauge felting needles; and a felting surface.

For The Tree Stump House You Will Need:

A cardboard kitchen roll tube; 1 mm wool felt in dark brown; PVA or fabric glue; an old paintbrush; carded wool in dark brown and white.
Optional Lantern: Natural acorn cap; amber-coloured glass bead; black wool felt; thin wire (22- or 24-gauge).

Curled-Up Hedgehog

Begin by making the long snout. Cut off a small corner from a sheet of cream merino pre-felt, and roll it up into a cone shape. Needle felt all over, and roll the tip between your fingers to create a thin point. To cover any joins, take a tiny amount of the cream pre-felt, tease it out with your fingers, then lay it over any joins in the snout and needle felt it into place.

Roll up dark-brown carded wool as tightly as you can, and then shape and needle felt it into a wide, kidney bean shape. Needle felt the base of the cone snout into the top section of the body. Tease out more cream pre-felt, and needle felt a forehead going down onto the snout. Use more pre-felt to create a cream belly and two little ears.

Cut four feet from 1 mm of the flesh wool felt, and use a fine-gauge needle to felt them on to your hedgehog.

You can use black or brown felt to make a tiny nose, and simply felt or glue it on, or try using a bit of 3D fabric paint.

Make two eyes sockets with your felting needle or an awl, and then glue in the stem-back eyes.

Walking Hedgehog

Make a snout the same way as before. Take a strip of dark-brown carded wool, and roll the thickest end of the snout up in it. Needle felt all over to anchor the snout inside the wool. Shape your hedgehog so the top is higher (wrap more wool around if necessary), and felt the base flatter.

Make more feet from wool felt, and needle felt them onto the underside of your hedgehog. Add the eyes and nose the same way as you did for the curled-up hedgehog.

Tree stump

Take the cardboard tube and trim a section off the top. Wrap brown, 1 mm wool felt (or pre-felt) around the tube to get the right size before cutting. Make sure the felt is wide enough to join together at the back and that it over laps the top of the cardboard tube by an inch or so. Cut a jagged edge across the top of the felt. Apply a generous amount of fabric or PVA glue to the cardboard tube, and wrap your cut felt fabric back around it.

When dry, draw on an arched doorway, and cut it out.

From the arch door cutout, cut strips and fold and cut them to make little branches for either side of the stump. Colour in any noticeable cardboard with a brown marker, then add 'flocking' by finely chopping brown wool felt until it's almost like powder, and then use fabric glue to stick it over any gaps in the branches. Glue the branches onto the sides of the tree, and then glue white carded wool on them for the snow. Draw on wood effect grain on the stump using a brown marker.

For the base, cut a circle of pre-felt, and needle felt brown carded wool onto it. Once completely covered in brown, hold your stump on top of the base to work out where you want the path to go, then felt white carded wool into place going around the back of the tree. Once you're happy with the tree's position, add glue around the bottom rim, and glue into place.

The Lantern
Cut two thin felt strips around 1.5 to 2 inches long, and glue each end to the inside of an acorn cap. Glue an amber or orange bead onto the felt, and wait for it to dry.
TIP: It might be easier to glue the bead to the felt strip and let dry before gluing into the acorn cap.

Next, glue on the other black strip in the opposite direction.

Place the lantern upside down onto your felting surface or sponge, and use a strong sewing needle to pierce a hole through your acorn cap. Thread wire through to create the hook, then hang the lantern onto the tree branch.

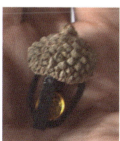

Finally, make a little sign from cardboard, colour it in with markers, and glue it above the arched door.

Sleepy Winter Mice

You Will Need:

Pipe cleaners; core wool; white carded wool; 1 mm wool felt in flesh and winter leaf shades of your choice; marker pens; white horsehair whiskers; needle and thread; pink embroidery skein for the tail; 38- and 36-gauge felting needles; a felting surface; and fabric glue or a hot glue gun.

Optional: Fabric paint and glitter glue.

Cut a white pipe cleaner to around 2 to 3 inches, and bend the tip over one half inch for the head. Wrap a thin strip of white carded wool around the neck and head area, and needle felt into place. Add more white wool to build up the body, leaving the head and neck area thinner. Cut any excess pipe cleaner from the bottom.

Cut out two little ear shapes following the template guide, fold each ear in half and needle felt through the base fold onto the sides of your mouse's head. Felt a little excess wool over the base of each ear to hold securely in place.

Colour the nose pink with a marker, and sew two black cotton stitches either side of the head for the sleeping eyes. Sew on a little mouth detail with one strand of black cotton.

Night Cap

For the cap, cut a small corner from a sheet of 1 mm thick felt, and draw a design onto it with a marker pen or fabric paint. (I have done blue stripes on mine with a marker pen.) Sew the two straight outer edges together using a blanket stitch. Finally, at an angle, sew white horse hair whiskers through the end of the nose, and trim to length. Secure the whiskers in place using a dab of super glue.

TIP: When gluing in whiskers, rather than applying to the nose or base area of the whisker, I like to apply the super glue to the whisker itself on one side, then pull the whisker through the nose from the other side so the glue goes through the nose and doesn't end up all over the wool.

The Leaves

Transfer leaf patterns on to 1 mm coloured wool felt using a fabric transfer pen. Cut out the felt leaf shapes, and if desired, keep them plain, or add detail with a marker pen or by decorating with fabric or glitter glue.

To make the tails, dip a length of pink embroidery skein into PVA glue/water solution, and bend the top to shape, and leave to dry. When dry, use a hot glue gun to glue the base of the tail onto the inside of the leaf, and glue the mouse's back on top of the tail. Lastly, roll the mouse up in the leaf and glue the leaf edges together.

Ear

Example leaf shape.

Squirrels & Acorns

You Will Need:

Pre-felt (Shetland); core wool; carded wool in grey and rust; 1 mm thick rust wool felt; and a 2 mm bead. For the acorns you will need carded wool in light browns/greens; natural acorn caps; 38- and 36-gauge felting needles; and a felting surface.

The head, body, and tail are made from one section. Measure out pre-felt 6 inches by 3 inches, and roll it up tightly. Measure out 1 inch for the head, 2 inches for the body, and 3 inches for the tail. Wrap a thin strip of core wool around the body and head, then needle felt into shape.

Felt a pinch of tan wool around the nose end, then a thin strip of grey wool around the head and body. Needle felt into place, adding more grey wool around the tail. Lightly roll the whole thing between the palms of your hands, and then redefine the head, body, and tail using your felting needle. Bend the end of the tail around, and felt through the bend until it stays in position.

30

The Legs

Cut thin strips of wool felt to make the legs. Needle felt one end, and roll between your fingers to form rounded paws. Dip only the paw ends into the PVA/water mixture, bend the back paws and legs into shape, and let dry.

When dry, wrap a bit of grey wool around the top of the legs, and needle felt until securely in place. Needle felt two small flat 'buns' for the back thighs. One at a time, needle felt the top of the back legs into position on either side of your squirrel, and felt the thighs over the top to hold the legs in place. Use a small amount of grey wool fibre to cover any joins onto the back and down onto the legs. Attach the front legs using more grey fibre.

Cut out the ears from tan wool felt, and use a fine-gauge needle to felt through the base of each ear onto the top of the head. Finally, colour the tip of the nose with a brown marker and add small, stem-back eyes.

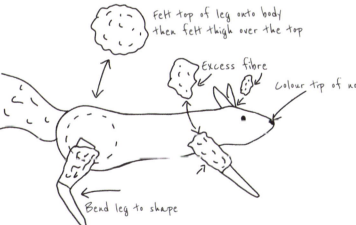

Felt top of leg onto body then felt thigh over the top

Excess fibre

Colour tip of nose

Bend leg to shape

Acorns

I like to use a mixture of browns and greens for the acorns. By blending wool colours together, you create more realism. Once you've felted an oval shape, roll it between the palms of your hand to shape and smooth further. Then simply glue one end into a natural acorn cap using fabric glue or a hot glue gun.

31

Eskimo

You Will Need:

Core wool; carded wool in white, tan and rust; pre-felt in black and flesh shades; wire and cotton thread for the fishing rod; blue felt or holographic spandex fabric for the fish; 38- and 36-gauge felting needles; and a felting surface.

Start by making the core body shape following the diagram as a guide. Next, spread out flesh-coloured pre-felt, and needle felt it over the face and head area. Needle felt black wool across the forehead for the fringe. (If you want to make a little girl Eskimo, you can make small plaits from black wool tops and felt them onto the sides of the head.)

Now wrap light-tan carded wool around the body, covering the base and over the top the head for the hood. Felt as evenly as possible, and add a good coverage of the tan wool on the back.

For the arms, needle felt a thin sausage shape using the tan wool, and vigorously roll it between the palms of your hands to smooth and even the shape. Needle felt rust-coloured carded wool around each end, then smooth out a strip of white, and felt on a 'fur' trim to each of the mittens.

Cut the arms in half to make two equal lengths, then attach them one at a time to the sides of your Eskimo's body. Use excess fibre over the shoulder join to hold the arms in place.

  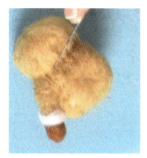 

Take more white wool, and needle felt and roll it to make a nice thin even strip. Use the strip to add 'fur' trim detail around the hood, base, and the front section of your Eskimo's coat.

Use a wisp of the flesh pre-felt, and roll it around between your fingers to make a ball-shaped nose. Use a fine-gauge needle to felt it into the centre of the face. Use thin black wool to 'draw' on two little lines for the eyes, and felt a dot of black wool for the mouth.

Finally, use more of the black wool to felt on small 'X' fastenings on front of the coat.

The Igloo

You Will Need:

Upholstery foam or a large bath sponge, and white and grey carded wool.

Take a square of upholstery foam, and cut bits off to make a dome shape. To make room for your battery lights, carefully cut out some of the foam from the underside, use your fingers to pull out the excess sponge/foam if it's easier. Cut out a small arch at the front for a door.

If needed, add a small amount of core wool to the top of the igloo to give the roof more height and a more rounded 'dome' shape. Needle felt on white carded wool a small section at a time.

Roll/tease out grey wool until it's very thin and use your needle to 'draw' on brick detail around the igloo.

Felt a separate strip of core wool, large enough so when you fold it into an arch, it covers the doorway neatly on your igloo. Once you have the right size, cover the strip in the same white carded wool and add a similar brick pattern/detail that you did on the rest of the igloo. Felt the grey brick detail around the sides of the arch strip too.

Use a hot glue gun to stick the arch over the doorway.

The Seal Pup

You Will Need:
White and grey carded wool; black pre-felt; 2 mm black stem-back eyes.

Needle felt a small 'ice cream cone' shape. Cover it in white carded wool by wrapping and felting the wool on a bit at a time. Roll the body between the palms of your hands.

Make a kind of heart shape snout from a tiny amount of grey wool and felt it upside down in the centre of your seals face.

Needle felt four little fin shapes from the same white wool used for covering the body. Needle felt the back fins either side of the pointy tail, and the other two fins either sides of the front lower body section.

Needle felt/roll between your fingers a small oval shape nose from black pre-felt and needle felt into place.
Make two eye sockets using your felting needle or awl tool and glue in the bead stem eyes.

The Sledge

You Will Need:
1 mm wool felt in grey/brown; gold embroidery thread; and a thin wire.

Cut out all of the components (as pictured opposite) from 1 mm brown/grey wool felt. Round off the base ski 'slats' with sharp scissors, and dip them in PVA/water solution. Wrap and shape the ends around a pencil to curve them. Dip all the other cut-out felt components in the PVA mixture, and leave to dry.

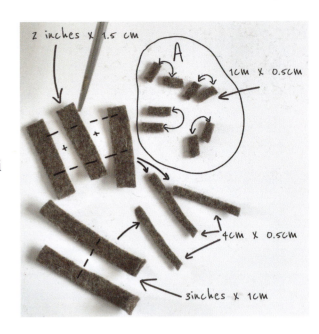

Glue one of the 4 cm thin strips across the two ski slats to join them (see picture opposite). Next, glue the small, 1 cm x 0.5 cm brackets as pictured in circle 'A' together, so that the eight become four. Use fabric glue to stick two of them upright on either side on the ski slats. Lay the 2 inch x 1.5 cm slats side by side, and glue the other two 4 cm thin bars across them to hold together. When dry, add fabric glue on top of the four upright brackets, and glue the top on.

Push and glue in a wire hook to the front middle section, and tie embroidery thread through it. Sew the other end through the mitten of your Eskimo.

The Foresters

You Will Need:

Core wool; coloured pre-felt in flesh and white; carded wool in neutral browns/greys and black; 1 mm wool felt in white and neutral tones; 3 mm black stem-bead eyes; 38- and 36-gauge felting needles; a felting surface; and fabric glue or a hot glue gun.

Optional: Scraps of lace/ribbon and curly wool yarn.

Needle felt a cone shape, but round it off at the top and flatten the base. Thin out flesh pre-felt using your fingers, and lay it flat over the top front head section, then needle felt it into place. Next, wrap carded wool of your choice around the body, also covering the base. If you're creating a male Forester, needle felt up through the bottom middle to give the impression of trousers. If you're making a woman, keep the base flat, as if it's a dress. Use darker-coloured wool to felt a belt around the body. If you're creating a woman, you can use ribbon or lace instead. Follow the stencil sheet as a guide.

Cut out a jagged beard shape, and a separate the little moustache from 1 mm thick wool felt. Felt a bit of black carded wool through the beard and onto the face; this should hold it in place. Roll a pinch of flesh pre-felt between your fingers to create a nose. Needle felt it through the top of the moustache and into the head to attach.

Needle felt a thin strip from the same colour wool you used to cover the body, and roll between the palms of your hands to make a sausage shape. Cut it in half so you have two equal lengths for the arms, and use a bit of fibre to secure the shoulders into the body.

Use wool felt to make a strip of hair, and cut the bottom edge jagged to match the beard. Needle felt the top edge around the top of the head. Roll two bits of felt to make two eyebrows, and glue in place with a dab of fabric glue. Make a cone-shaped hat out of felt following the guide on the stencil page, and glue onto the top of the head.

TIP: Natural pre-felt makes great hair, as it's slightly thicker and has more texture than other felt. You can also use wool yarn or curly locks to make the hair and beard.

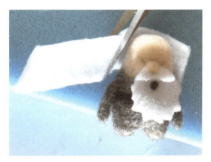

You can use pre-felt to make bunches by using the hair bunches temple on the stencil page. Needle felt the middle section onto the top of the head to make the parting, roll both ends between your fingers to form points, and then tie a ribbon bow on either side. *Why not make a whole family of Foresters!*

Flesh pre-felt

Carded wool

Cut in half to make the arms

Glue lace apron

Glue on ribbon band

Nose/unfolded

Sew

Cone hat

Sew

Bunches

Needle felt through the middle onto top of head

Tie ribbon

Mens hair

Toadstool Tealight House

You Will Need:

Cardboard roll; carded wool in brown, red, orange, white; white pre-felt; 1 mm wool felt in tan, black, and brown; needle and thread; 38- and 36-gauge felting needles; a felting surface; and fabric glue or a hot glue gun.

Optional: Paper-covered wire and beads.

Use brown carded wool to felt a 'burger bun'–shaped roof, approximately 5 to 6 inches in diameter. Felt orange wool around the top edges, leaving some of the brown showing, then felt red on top of that, leaving some of the orange showing. Felt white spots, in various sizes, all over the roof.

For the chimney, cut out a strip of black felt just over an inch high, and roll it up. Cut a small circle of black felt, and cut out a small 'V' dart. Overlap and glue the dart edges together, then glue it on top of the chimney cylinder. Needle felt an indentation into your roof, and glue the base of the chimney into it.

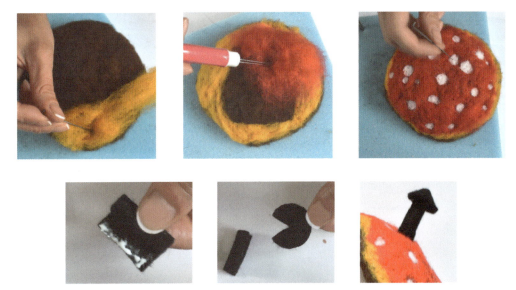

Using fabric glue, glue white pre-felt around the cardboard tube. Add glue on the inside rim, and fold the edges under to neaten. When dry, cut out an arched door. Use the excess cutout arch as a template to make a new door from brown felt. If desired, sew or glue on a small bead for a door handle. Use a couple of stitches as hinges to hold the felt door in place on the house. Cut green paper-covered wire, and push one end through the side of the house, and then bend into a hook to hang a small bead lantern.

Use a craft knife to carefully cut out a window, then cut a window frame from brown felt, and glue it on. You can add as many windows as you wish! The more windows, the more magical it will look when you add the battery lights later.

Decorate the outside of the house by gluing on embroidery thread and small felt leaf shapes.
TIP: Use a cocktail stick to apply the glue.

Needle felt a flat disc base from brown carded wool approximately 6 inches in diameter. Hold your house in position on the base so you can work out where you want a path to go, and needle felt white wool on either side and round the back of the house. Don't glue your house to the base, as you want it to be removable so you can add tea lights underneath.

To make a fence on either side, cut two thin strips of brown felt, the length of the path from the door to the edge of the base.
TIP: Stiffen your strips of felt using starch or PVA glue/water solution before you cut.

Cut more thin strips of felt for the upright fence posts. Cut each post to a point, then glue into place. When dry, add fabric glue to the base of each post, and glue the fence on either side of the path. If desired, needle felt white wool over the roof for a snowy effect.

2D Magical Winter Castle

You Will Need:

White pre-felt; coloured wool fibre (either tops or carded wool) in yellow, peach, tan, dark grey, medium grey, black, dark teal/blue, dark brown, medium brown, lilac, light blue, and white; fabric transfer pen; 38- and 36-gauge felting needles; and a felting surface.
Optional: Angelina fibres and fabric glue.

Begin by tracing the template using a fabric transfer marker. Lay the paper image facedown on the pre-felt, and iron over the reverse side until the stencil is transferred.

I generally add colours 'dark to light', but I find it easier to create the light sky background first. Begin by felting the peach and light-yellow wool onto the sky area, felting around and between the trees and castle.

Add the same colours into the lake for the reflection of the sky.

NOTE: I used a slightly lighter colour yellow for the water reflection.

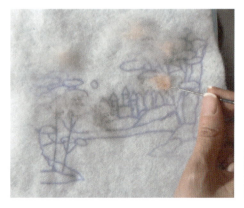
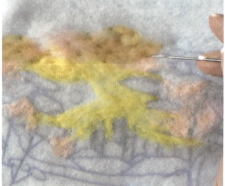

Colour the rest of the picture using the 'Felt by Numbers Guide' on the stencil page, laying down the dark wool first. Once the dark colours are in place, felt a thin layer of white wool for the snow over the hills. I sometimes find it easier to needle felt pictures by first felting on an outline of fibre around all the shapes in the design.

Needle felt dark brown for the trees.

If desired, leave the trees dark brown, or add white wool on top for a snowy effect.

Use heat-bondable Angelina fibres for the shimmering lake and castle detail. Smooth out some Angelina fibres onto a flat work surface, cover with a sheet of baking paper or plain A4 writing paper, and iron over the paper for a few seconds until the Angelina fibres have bonded together. Peel the bonded fibres off of the paper, and spread out over your lake. Cut to shape, and use your needle to tuck any stray fibres around the edges of the lake.

NOTE: As Angelina fibres do not felt into wool very well, I tend to use a small amount of fabric glue here and there to fix them in place.

For the castle detail, cut small strips and triangle shapes of bonded Angelina fibres, and glue them onto your castle.

I used a black marker to draw the door, windows, and brick detail on top of the Angelina fibre castle.

I usually like to sew in flying birds using a single strand of embroidery thread, but here I simply used a thin amount of wool and a fine-gauge needle to needle felt them into place.

Finally, felt in a few brown curly locks to the foreground.

Magical Winter Castle Stencil

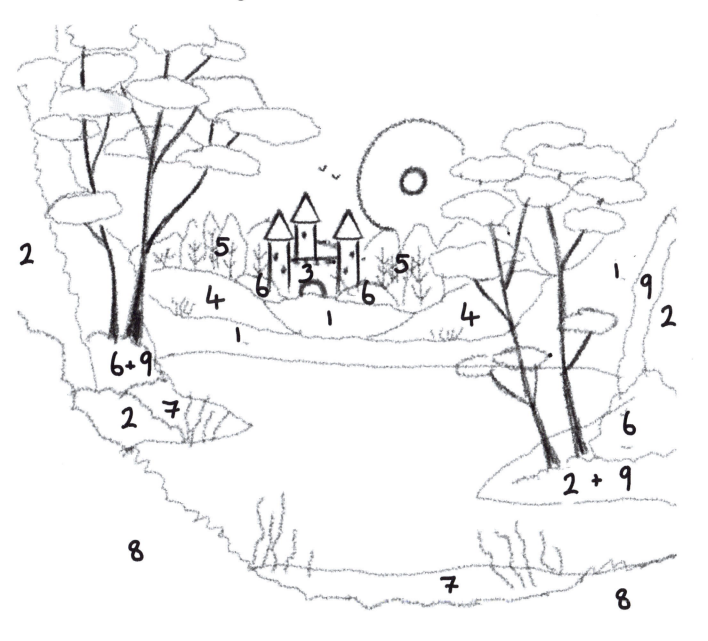

2D Sleeping Fox & Butterflies

Try felting this little fox picture using the same principle for the castle picture.

Use a fabric pen to transfer the image below onto pre-felt. Start by felting the black ears, then add the light-rust colours, followed by the white, and then the dark grey and browns on the tail. I needle felted an outline with thin strips of black wool and added light-blue wool in the ear and to separate the tail from the face.

Another Idea: You can also print off and trace around pictures of moths and butterflies using the fabric transfer pen. Transfer the outline to wool felt, and needle felt on the detail using coloured wool, following the photos as a guide. Then add bits of lace to add detail to their delicate wings.

Winter King

You Will Need:

Core wool; felting wool in white, dark grey, light grey, dark brown (I used carded wool); flesh-coloured pre-felt; white, 1 mm wool felt; small stem-bead eyes; Wensleydale curly locks in white; pipe cleaner; wire; 38- and 36-gauge felting needles; needle and thread; a felting surface; and fabric glue.
Optional: Silver embroidery thread and a crystal bead.

Start by needle felting a cone shape approximately 5 to 6 inches high with a 3- to 4-inch base. Needle felt the base flat. Use sharp scissors or an awl to make a hole through the top (this is for the arms to go through). For the arms, cut a pipe cleaner to approximately 6 inches in length, fold the tips of each end over, and tightly pinch together. Push the pipe cleaner through the hole, making sure your arms are even lengths on either side. Wrap white carded wool tightly around each arm, and needle felt to secure. Needle felt more wool around the armpit join to cover it.

Needle felt more white wool over the rest of the body, then needle felt grey detail to the front. Use very thin dark brown wool to felt three X's down the front. Wrap dark-grey wool around each hand, and needle felt into place. Round off the ends of each hand to resemble mittens. Take a thin strip of cream wool and roll it between your fingers, wrap it around the base of each mitten to create the look of a fur trim, and needle felt into place.

The Head

Needle felt a ball using core wool approximately 1 inch in diameter. Smooth flesh-coloured pre-felt over the face, and felt it around to secure it at the back and sides of the head. Needle felt Wensleydale locks into the top 'parting' of the head, one section at a time.

Needle felt more Wensleydale locks lightly together to form a beard.

Place the beard onto the face, and work out where you want the mouth to go, then needle felt a pinch of black wool through the beard and onto the face to secure the beard. Adding the little black mouth forms the impression of the moustache.

Take a pinch of flesh pre-felt and needle felt and roll it with your fingers to shape a small nose. Needle felt the nose onto the face, then work out your king's eye position. Push your needle (or awl) right through the head to create the eye sockets, then one at a time, glue in the bead stem-back eyes. Make a white felt crown using the template on the stencil page, then if desired, sew a star pattern onto the crown using silver embroidery thread. You can sew the matching pattern onto the top of each mitten.

Use a cocktail stick to make a hole in the base of the head, then glue the other end of the cocktail stick down into the king's body. Add fabric glue to the tip of the exposed cocktail stick, and push the head back on.

To make his magic stick, wrap a length of wire (approximately 6 inches) with a thin strip of brown merino tops. Needle felt it around the wire to secure in place. Dip the wool-covered wire in PVA/water solution and let it dry. Bend the top over into a curved 'hook' shape, and sew a crystal bead through it.

Cape Stencil

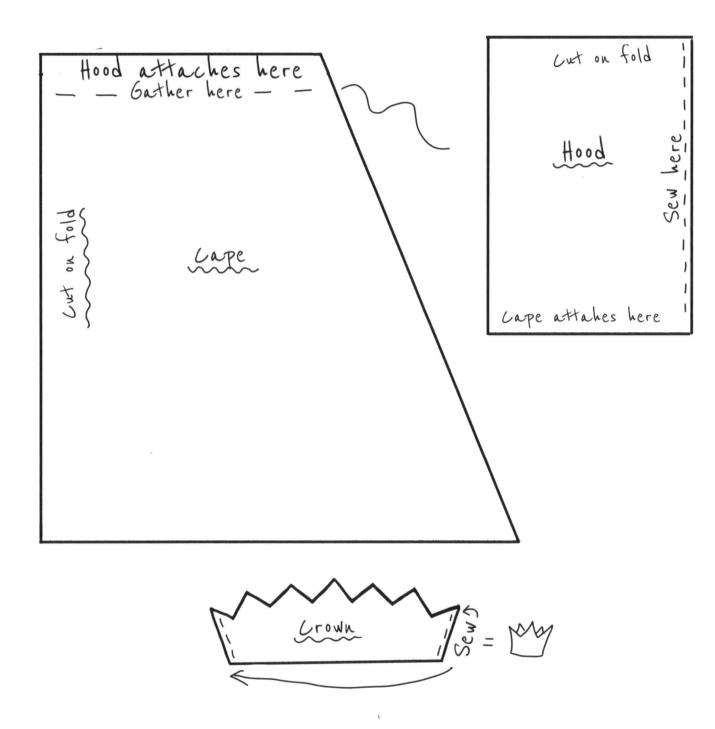

Cut the stencil shapes out of pre-felt or wool felt. Sew the two edges of the hood together using a backstitch or a blanket stitch, and turn right way out.

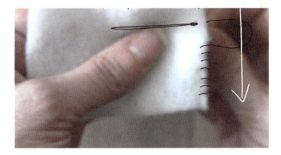 

Sew a running stitch across the top of the cape using embroidery thread, and leave a length at each end so you can tie around your king later. Sew the bottom of the hood to the top of the cape section.

If desired, needle felt a fur trim around the edges using carded wool. Tie the cape around your king's neck.

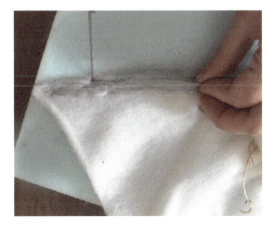 

Hanging decorations

Hanging Decorations

You Will Need:

Toadstools:
Red pre-felt; white pre-felt; carded white wool; needle and thread; glue; 38- and 36-gauge felting needles; and a felting surface. Optional: Curly locks.

Walnuts:
Cream pre-felt (I used Shetland); carded wool in tan, light brown, and dark brown; a needle and thread.

To make the tops of the toadstools, cut out a circle from your chosen colour pre-felt.
Cut out two triangular 'darts' on either side, and slightly overlap the edges. Needle felt into place.

Using your fingers, tease out more pre-felt (in the same colour), and use a fine-gauge needle to felt over the joins.

TIP: It helps to felt over the joins if you put your mushroom cap over a corner of your felting sponge.

Take bits of white carded wool and needle felt them into little 'spots' on your mushroom cap. Trim off any excess fuzz from the underside.

Next, thread a needle with embroidery thread or cotton of your choice, and double up the thread, tying a knot in the end. Sew up through the middle underside of your mushroom cap, then tie another knot (leaving enough length for a hoop), and cut the excess thread.

For the stem, tightly roll a square piece of cream pre-felt into a cylinder, and needle felt all over to secure.

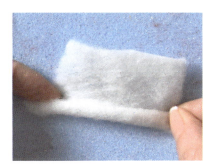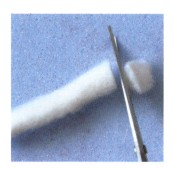

Cut the base to neaten, and if desired, needle felt white curly locks over the top. (I used Bluefaced Leicester.)

Last, glue the top of the stem into the middle underside of the cap.

Walnuts:

Use an A4 size sheet of Shetland wool pre-felt. Measure approximately 1.5 inches in from one corner, and cut a strip (at an angle) down the longest side. Starting at the thickest end, tightly roll the cut strip so you're left with an oval shape. Needle felt all over to secure.

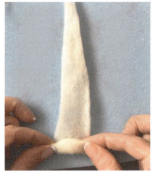

Cover the oval shape with light-tan carded wool, and then needle felt little bumpy lines using a medium-brown wool.

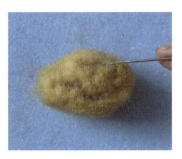

Needle felt a strip of the tan wool, and roll it between your fingers to smooth the fibres.
Needle felt it into place around the middle section of your walnut. Use your fingers to pinch the middle section of your walnut further into shape.

Next, needle felt a very thin strip of dark brown wool around the middle section of your walnut.

Finally, sew in a hoop as you did for the mushroom cap.

You Will Need:

Core wool; carded wool in white, grey, and black; 1 mm grey wool felt; pipe cleaners; 3 mm black bead stem eyes; 38- and 36-gauge felting needles; a felting surface; and fabric glue.

Use the stencil page as a guide for the size and shapes of the body parts. When making the head, you may think that the core shape appears too small, but by the time you add the top coat wool, it should be just right.

Head

Make the round head and body shape from core wool.

Needle felt the snout separately using only the white carded wool, and felt the end firmly into place on the core wool head. Wrap more white wool around the top section of the snout, covering the join area on the head. Needle felt into place.

Wrap grey wool around the head, leaving the snout area white.
Felt a thin strip of grey down the middle of the nose. Then felt more white onto the lower sides of the head to create fuzzy cheeks. Trim the cheeks to shape using sharp scissors.

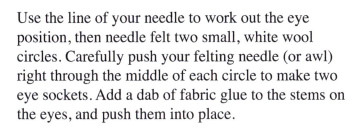

Use the line of your needle to work out the eye position, then needle felt two small, white wool circles. Carefully push your felting needle (or awl) right through the middle of each circle to make two eye sockets. Add a dab of fabric glue to the stems on the eyes, and push them into place.

Needle felt an oval shape from either black wool or black pre-felt. Roll it between your fingers to smooth and shape a nose. Needle felt one point of the oval into place, then fold the top half down and felt the two points together.

 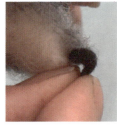 

Cut out the ears from 1 mm grey wool felt, and needle felt a fine amount of grey carded wool over them. Felt the wool over the edges and onto the other side of the wool felt. Needle felt white detail into the middle of each ear using a thin strip of white carded wool.

One at a time, position the ears onto the back/top section of the head, and use more grey fibre to attach through the base of the ears onto the head. Now needle felt a small strip of the grey wool between the ears to build up the forehead a little more. This keeps the ears correctly spaced.

Body

Once you have needle felted the body shape from core wool, cover the font section with the white carded wool. Needle felt through the top section of the back and into the back of the head. Cover the back and neck area with grey wool, and felt white up under the neck area to cover the join. Your wolf will look more inquisitive if you position the head at a slight angle before attaching.

Legs

Cut your pipe cleaner into four lengths following the guide on the 'Wolf Stencil Page'.

Tightly wrap thin strips of white carded wool around each leg, and needle felt into place. Felt around the paws to neaten and round them off. Now roll each wool-covered leg between the palms of your hands. Wrap more white wool around the thigh area on the back legs, and needle feet into place.

Felt the tops of the front legs into the chest area of your wolf. Make sure the paws touch the ground so your wolf sits and balances well. Once you are certain of the position, needle felt more white wool over the tops of the legs firmly into the chest area to secure in place.

Position the back legs, and one at a time, needle felt through the thigh area to anchor them on. Once happy with the position, needle felt the grey wool through each thigh. Leave the front area of the thighs white.

Needle felt a tail using the carded white wool, and felt grey wool onto the top section of it.

Trim off any grey fuzz from the underside of the tail, then needle felt one end onto the bottom mid-back section of your wolf. Needle felt more grey wool over the join area, going slightly up your wolf's back.

Curl the tail around the side of your wolf, and needle felt it all over until it stays in place.

Last, give your wolf a trim using sharp scissors.

The Wolf - Stencil

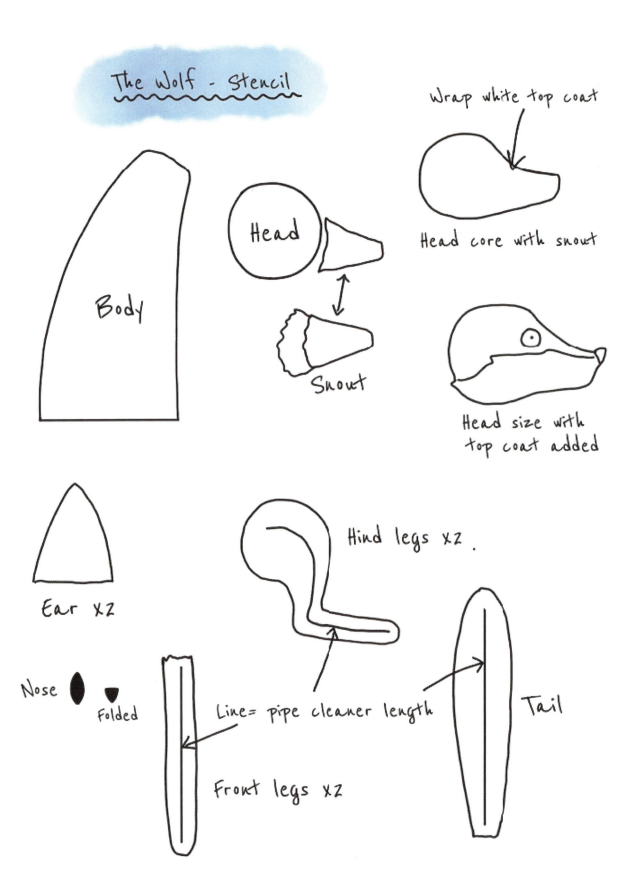

Wrap white top coat

Head core with snout

Head

Snout

Head size with top coat added

Body

Ear x2

Hind legs x2.

Nose ● ▼ Folded

Line= pipe cleaner length

Front legs x2

Tail

Ice Bear

You Will Need:
Core wool; white carded wool; black pre-felt; 3 mm black stem-bead eyes; 38- and 36-gauge felting needles; a felting surface; and fabric glue.

Head and Body
Begin by needle felting the head from core wool using the head shape on the stencil page as a guide. Needle felt a circle first, then felt more across the forehead and cheeks so the snout is left protruding out. Needle felt the body shape, and then felt more core wool across the lower back section of the bear's body to build it up.

Position the head at the top of the body (slightly towards the front), and needle felt more core wool over the join at the back of the head, or the top of body, to attach the head securely.

Now needle felt a light coverage of white carded top coat wool all over the head and body section.

Legs

Needle felt thick sausage shapes for the legs, following the guide on the stencil page. Roll them vigorously between the palms of your hands to help shape. Fold the paws up, and needle felt through the bend to secure the position.

One at a time, position the legs onto the side of your bear, making sure that the paws reach the floor, then felt firmly through the top of the leg section into the body.

Needle felt two separate shoulder sections from the same white carded wool, and one at a time, felt them over the top of the leg area and onto the top of the back, so they meet. This gives a nice little 'hump' to your bear's back. If needed, felt more of the white carded top coat over any joins in the shoulder area.

Make the back legs from the same white carded wool, and follow the guide on the stencil page for the size and shape. Needle felt the back legs onto the back end of the bear's body.
TIP: Look from beneath your bear to get an even position for the back legs.

Needle felt a tail shape, and felt more wool fibre up through the base of your bear's bottom.

Needle felt two round ears using your fingers to carefully 'fold' over the edges as you felt.

Position each ear at the sides of the head, slightly towards the back, and needle felt through the base to attach them. If needed, felt more fibre over any noticeable joins.

I like to felt thin black wool onto the paws to define the 'toes'. It's up to you if you want to do this, or if prefer, you can sew the detail on using black cotton.

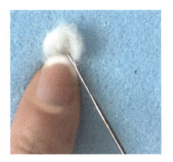   

Make a black nose from either black pre-felt or black or dark-brown carded wool. Roll it between your fingers to form an oval shape, and attach it to the snout the same way as I explained for the wolf.

Use the line of your needle to work out the eye position, then make two eye sockets using your felting needle or awl, and glue in black stem-back eyes.

Finally, if desired, sew on the mouth detail, and give your bear a trim using sharp scissors.

Ice Bear Stencil

Body

Head/Side view

Head/Birdseye view

Add wool to build up the lower back

X

Nose

Body/Side view

Back leg } x2

Bend & felt here for foot

Ear x 2

Front leg x } 2

Bend & felt here for paw

Stag Brooch

You Will Need:

Merino tops wool in light blue, medium blue, and white; carded wool in brown and cream; pre-felt in dark brown and black; 3 mm black bead eyes; needle and thread; 1 mm wool felt; a l arge safety pin; 38- and 36-gauge felting needles; a felting surface; and fabric glue.

I tend not use merino tops that often, but I find it does work really well for making these brooch backs. First, pull (don't cut) medium to dark-blue merino wool into strips, and then lay them on top of each other in a crisscross direction.

TIP: If you want to, you can felt the wool inside of a cookie cutter to get an even circle shape more quickly, or you can cut a circle out of pre-felt and felt the merino tops onto it. I have chosen to do it freehand here. **You want the circle to be around three inches in diameter.** I find it quicker to use the multi-pronged felting tool for this part. Use it to carefully 'drag' over the edges as you felt into shape. Needle felt until the merino becomes as solid as you can get it, and once you're happy with the circle shape, ues a thin, light-blue merino tops, and needle felt it over the top.

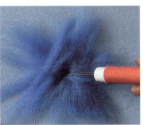

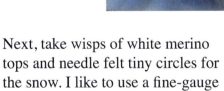

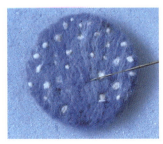

Next, take wisps of white merino tops and needle felt tiny circles for the snow. I like to use a fine-gauge needle for doing this.

The Stag

Cut a pipe cleaner to approximately 2.5 inches in length, and for the head, fold one end over about half an inch. Tightly wrap a thin strip of cream carded wool around the head and nose section, and then needle felt it into place. You may need to wrap more cream wool around the nose tip, but try to keep the nose area fairly narrow. If needed, use the guide on the 'Stag Brooch' stencil page for the sizes and shapes.

Next, wrap thin strips of medium-brown carded wool around the top section of the head and down onto the neck. Use your fingers to help shape and bend the nose area up.

Needle felt two circles of cream carded wool on either side of the head for the eye socket detail.
NOTE: You may wish to needle felt the cream eye detail on later, after you've added the bead eyes.

Make a black nose by cutting a tiny corner of black pre-felt. Needle felt it into a heart -shape at the end of the nose. Then take a threadlike bit of the black wool, and felt on a tiny mouth directly beneath the nose.
NOTE: You may wish to sew this on using black cotton instead.

Once the nose is in place, needle felt a bit of light-brown carded wool just on the top bridge area of the nose, leaving the side areas white. Next, sew in 3 mm black bead eyes using the 'How to Sew in Eyes' guide on page 76.

Antlers
I made the antlers out of wool pre-felt.

Cut a thin strip of pre-felt, and needle felt it all over just a little. Roll the strip between your fingers to smooth it. Make another strip the same way, and cut it into four smaller strips. One by one, needle felt the middle area of each smaller strip onto the larger strip as pictured.

Now carefully smooth PVA/water solution using your fingers to shape the horns. Once you're happy with the shape, leave to dry.

NOTE: You can also make horns in a similar way, but rather than needle felt the smaller strips on first, dip all the horn pieces in the glue/water mixture separately, let dry, then glue or tie them around the main horn strip.

While the antlers are drying, needle felt two ears using the stencil ear shape as a guide for the size. Add white carded wool into the middle part of each ear, and then pinch the ears between your fingers to help shape them.

TIP: You can always cut the ears out of brown wool felt or pre-felt.

Once the antlers are dry, use more of the brown carded wool to attach the middle section by needle felting over and into the top of the head.

One at a time, needle felt the ears into position, just below the base of each antler. Felt the excess fibre at the bottom of each ear onto the back of the head, then needle felt around the base of the ears to shape and neaten them.

Using a very thin strip of dark brown wool, needle felt brown detail just below the bead eyes, going into the corners and slightly down onto the sides of the face.

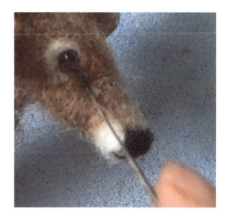

Attach the long neck area of your stag to the brooch back using the same brown carded wool. Needle felt firmly, working in small sections, until the stag is securely in place.

To enable the brooch back to have a safety pin clasp, measure and cut a circle of wool felt in your chosen colour, approximately the same size as the felted circle. Then cut a small square patch of the same colour felt, large enough to fit over the back bar of your safety pin. Position the safety pin onto the middle section of the felt circle, making sure that the opening is faced upwards. Use embroidery thread or thick cotton to sew the square patch in place.

Finally, glue the wool felt circle (with the clasp) to the back of the felted piece.

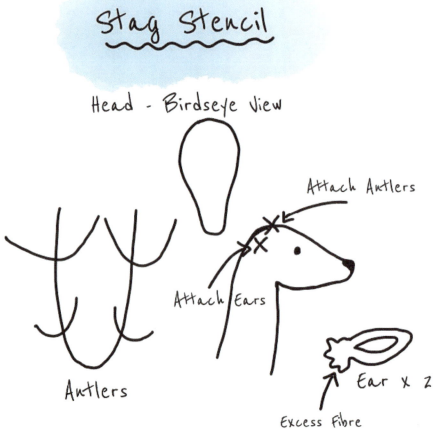

Stag Stencil

Head - Birdseye View

Attach Antlers

Attach Ears

Antlers

Ear x 2

Excess Fibre

Snow Leopard

You Will Need: Standard-length pipe cleaners (I like to use cotton pipe cleaners); core wool; cream or white carded top coat wool (I use a Bergschaf/merino blend); merino pre-felt in black and pink shades; 5 mm plastic or glass cat doll eyes (Alternatively, you can create a sleeping snow Leopard by felting a thin line of wool for the sleeping eyes, and once made, pose your Leopard so he is laying down in a curled up position); 38- and 36-gauge felting needles; fabric glue; white horse hair whiskers (optional); and an awl tool.

Hints and Tips

The assembled pipe cleaner frame is also perfect for making miniature cats. However, you would need to scale down the head and narrow the legs for a domestic cat. Bend the tips of the cut pipe cleaner over, and pinch together with a pair of pliers. This prevents the wire from the pipe cleaner poking through the wool later.

Cats can be very tricky. I think this is because they have a flat face, unlike dogs that have long snout areas.

A useful tip for a cat's features is to try not overdo it with the core wool. Just felt the main head shape using the stencil sheet as a guide. Then use a little more core wool to create a bridge strip for the nose, a strip across the top of the head, and a small chin. That's basically it.

Start by building your snow leopard's skeleton/frame using standard pipe cleaners. Measure them to length, and bend into shape following the stencil sheet.

Next, begin wrapping thin strips of your white topcoat wool around the bottom section of the legs, also going around the paws. Wrap as smoothly as you can, and use the back of your nail to help wrap neatly around the paws. Needle felt into place. Wrap more thin strips around the top areas of the legs, trying to keep all four legs even in size. Round off the front area of each paw with your felting needle, and then pinch the paws flat between your fingers to help shape them.

Using strips of core wool, start wrapping the body and neck. Needle felt on more strips of wool to build up the body.

Wrap a thinner strip around the nose. These will become the two front cheeks on your snow leopard. Needle felt another strip of core wool around the top section of the head, leaving a small section of the snout protruding.

Needle felt more strips of core wool around the bottom area, going in crisscross directions underneath the belly.

Now needle felt a separate section of core wool approximately 3 inches long by 1.5 inches wide. Needle felt it onto the underside of your snow leopard. Needle felt another section of core wool for the chest area, and needle felt it in between the front legs, going slightly up onto the underside of the neck.

Make two flat thigh shapes using the stencil sheet as a guide, and one at a time, needle felt them to the top of the back legs. Wrap a little more core wool around the join area of the thigh section.

Wrap topcoat wool around the tail, and needle felt into place.

Building the Face

Needle felt the underside of the head a little flatter.

Make a little nose/bridge strip, and needle felt it into the centre of the face. Define the small front cheeks and mouth area with your felting needle, as well as with your fingers. Needle felt a small strip of core wool, and felt it across the top front area of the head, creating the forehead. Spread out a sparse amount of white topcoat wool, lay it over the face, and needle felt it on, making sure you redefine the features.

Use an awl or fine knitting needle to create two eye sockets, then glue in each plastic stem teddy bear or cat eyes. Needle felt black wool around each eye.

Cut out the eyelids from cream pre-felt, and needle felt above the eyes so they slightly overlap the top of each eye.

Roll a bit of pink pre-felt between your fingers to shape it into an oval. Needle felt it sideways onto the end of the nose/bridge section. You may find there is a slight gap, so simply take a bit of the white top coat wool, smooth it horizontally across, and needle felt it into place. Needle felt two nostrils.

Tease some black wool until it's thread thin, then use your felting needle to 'draw' on the mouth. To help bring out the features, take a strong sewing needle, insert it into the chin area, and carefully 'pull' the wool forwards into shape.

Spread out the white top coat wool, and working in sections, needle felt it onto the body. Take your time to make sure the tops of the legs and any joins are well covered with the topcoat wool.

Turn your leopard upside down, and cover the tummy with topcoat wool.
Use more wool to cover over any gaps around the underside leg area. Take light grey or taupe-coloured wool, and needle felt a sparse covering all over the back, on the top side of the tail, down the outside of the legs, and over the top of the head.

Cut out two black ears from pre-felt and follow the ear stencil. Needle felt white topcoat wool into the middle of each ear, followed by more of the black on top of that. Trim off any excess fluff at the back of each ear using sharp scissors.

Needle felt the ears to the top of the head.

TIP: To work out a good position for the ears, view the head from above, and set the ears back at least 1 cm from the front edge of the forehead.
Needle felt a bit more of the taupe wool over the base of each ear to securely attach them.

Adding the Spots
Break up bits of black pre-felt into various sizes, and using a fine-gauge needle, felt them into spots all over your snow leopard's pelt.

Add black all around the tip of the tail. Felt thin black lines on the paws to create the effect of the toes. I usually start with the middle toe first, and then felt another line on either side.

If desired, sew in horse hair whiskers.

TIP: I find it best to add a dab of super glue onto the one side of the whiskers, near to the nose, and then pull the whiskers from the other side so the glue and whiskers go into the wool. That way, you avoid the super glue going onto the nose area.

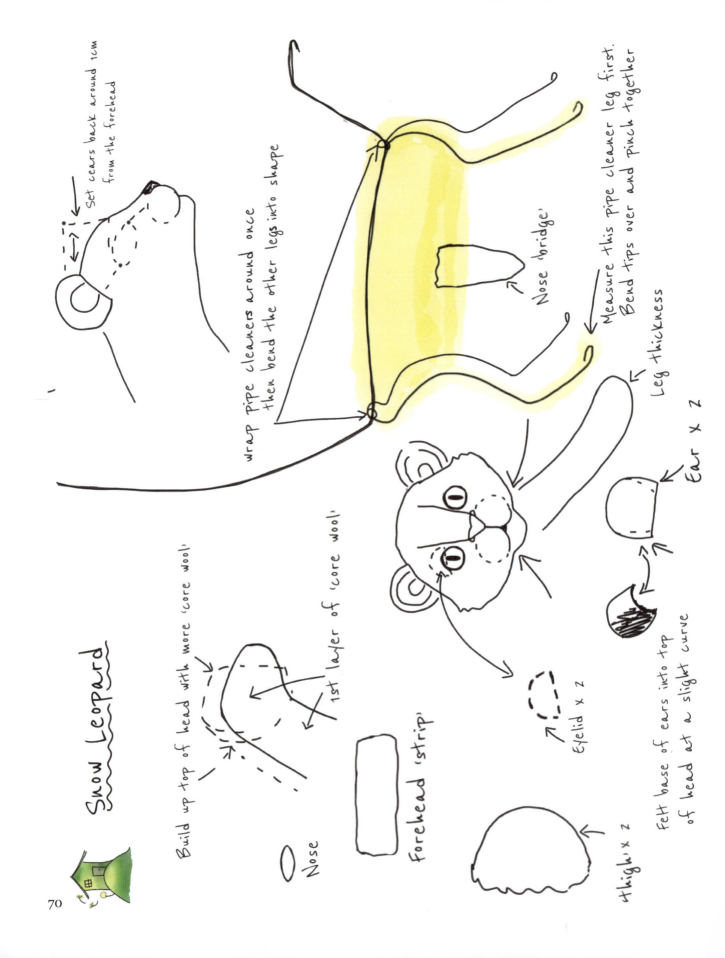

Snow Leopard

Set ears back around 1cm from the forehead

Wrap pipe cleaners around once then bend the other legs into shape

Nose 'bridge'

Measure this pipe cleaner leg first. Bend tips over and pinch together

Leg thickness

Ear x 2

Build up top of head with more 'core wool'

1st layer of 'core wool'

Nose

Forehead 'strip'

Eyelid x 2

Felt base of ears into top of head at a slight curve

Thigh x 2

The Arctic Fox

Needle felt the head and body from core wool. Use the measurements of wool as suggest on the stencil sheet. Shape the back of the body and head sections until they are rounded. Then needle felt the front body area until it's considerably flatter than the bottom area. Felt a semi-circle to define the thigh.

Needle felt the snout from white carded wool, and then attach the end of the snout onto the head. Felt white carded wool across the join, up onto the forehead.

Create the cheeks by needle felting small strips of the carded wool along the bottom edges of the snout and onto the sides of the head.

Make a nose the same as you did for the wolf.

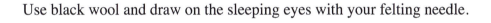
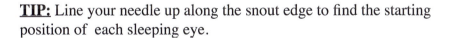

Use black wool and draw on the sleeping eyes with your felting needle.

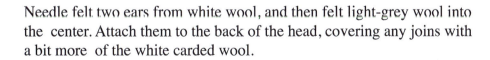

TIP: Line your needle up along the snout edge to find the starting position of each sleeping eye.

Needle felt two ears from white wool, and then felt light-grey wool into the center. Attach them to the back of the head, covering any joins with a bit more of the white carded wool.

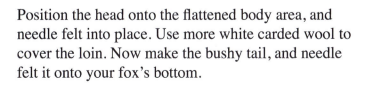

Position the head onto the flattened body area, and needle felt into place. Use more white carded wool to cover the loin. Now make the bushy tail, and needle felt it onto your fox's bottom.

71

Sleeping Arctic Fox stencil

head

1.5 grams of wool

ear x 2

felt the front area flatter

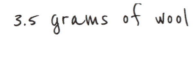

body

3.5 grams of wool

nose

nose/folded

tail

snout

The Majestic Snowshoe Hare

Begin by making the shapes for the body and head from core wool. Needle felt the top section of the body to the front area of the bottom body section so that it overlaps slightly. Felt a little more core wool around the join to hold the two sections together.

Cover the body in a thin layer of white carded wool.

Needle felt the nose area so that it tapers in. Use your fingers to help shape it further. Needle felt the top section of the head to make it slightly narrower, and then pinch the lower cheeks to make them chubby.

TIP: If you over felt an area of wool, or, for example, you want a nose to stick out more, insert a strong sewing needle horizontally, and then pull the features back out.

Make the ears from white carded wool, and needle felt some light grey wool in the centre of each ear. Attach the ears to the back of the head, positioning them close together and facing forwards.
Needle felt white carded wool around the back of the head, covering the base of the ears to keep them in place. Then needle felt a light covering of white carded wool over the rest of the head.

Work out the eye position on the sides of the head, and needle felt that area inwards to create a small socket. Sew in black, 3 mm, glass bead eyes.

Use thin, black carded wool to draw a V-shaped nose with your needle. Draw a mouth using more black wool.

For the front legs, cut a pipe cleaner to length using the stencil sheet, and one at a time, tightly wrap the legs with white carded wool. Vigorously roll each leg between the palms of your hands to help compress the wool around the pipe cleaner. Position the legs onto the hare's chest area, and make sure they're long enough to reach the ground and in line with the bottom of your hare. This will ensure he balances evenly. Needle felt more carded wool over the tops of the legs to hold them securely in place.

Make the back feet from small, wrapped pipe cleaner pieces, and needle felt them to the underside of the hare's bottom

To attach the head, first anchor it onto the top of the body using a blanket stitch, then needle felted white carded wool all the way around the neck area.

TIP: Position the head towards the back of the top section so the chest area is more pronounced.
Make the tail, and needle felt it underneath the bottom.

position head here

felt legs onto the chest

Snowhare stencil

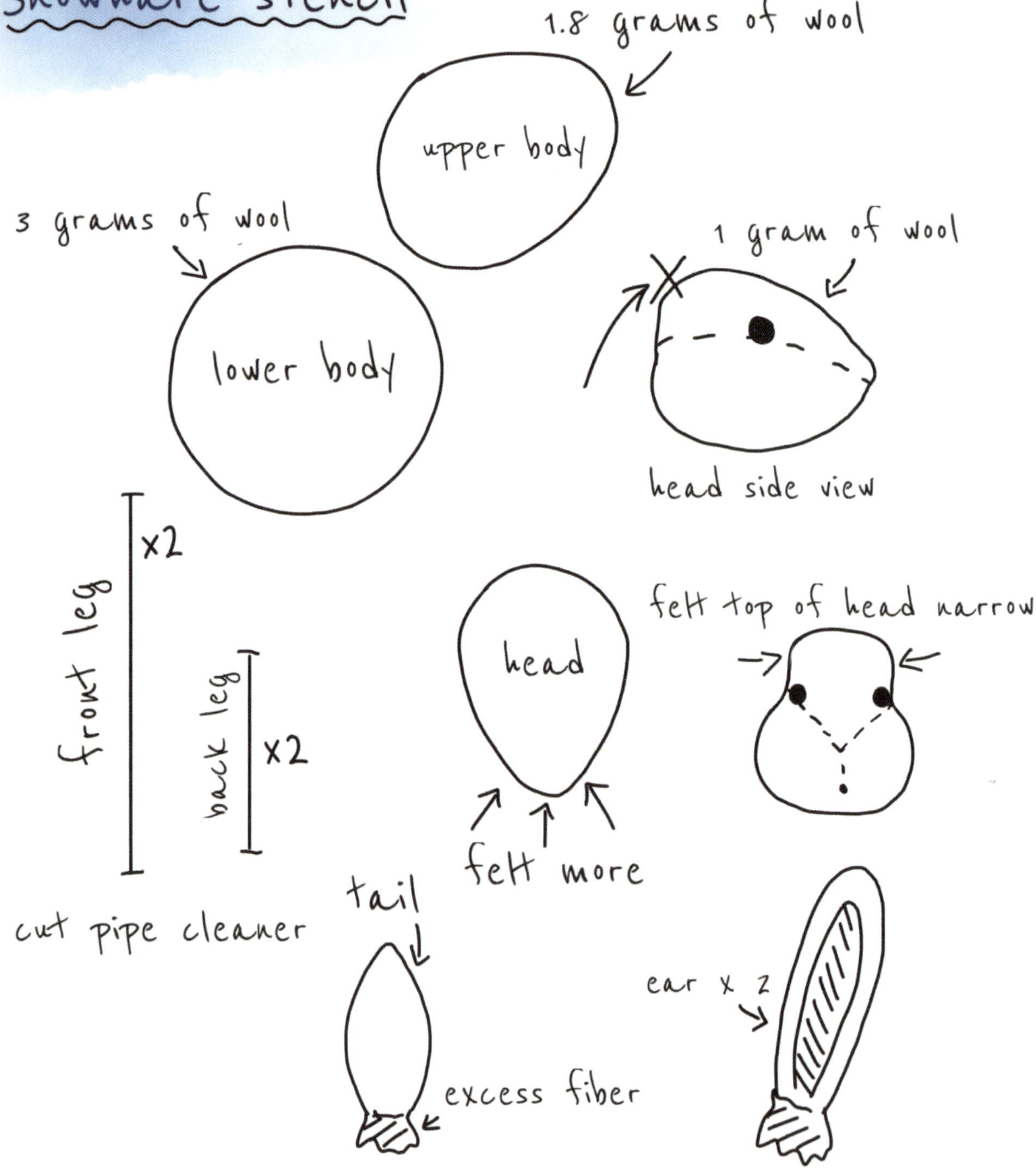

1.8 grams of wool

upper body

3 grams of wool

lower body

1 gram of wool

head side view

front leg | x2

back leg | x2

cut pipe cleaner

head

felt top of head narrow

felt more

tail

excess fiber

ear x 2

I'm going to leave you with this last cuddly project. I really do hope you've enjoyed making the projects in this book, whether they are for your own enjoyment or to give as gifts to your loved ones.

Wishing you a warm and woolly winter!

Rachel
xx

Mother and Baby Snuggly Badgers

Now that you've had some experience with the other designs, this one is completely down to you. Use the stencil page as a guide. I sewed the baby badger's head in place by anchoring on a blanket stitch beneath his head and sewing it in place onto the mother's body. You can use fabric glue to attach it if you prefer.

You Will Need:
Core wool; carded wool in grey, white, and black; needle and thread; 38- and 36-gauge felting needles, and a felting surface.

Mother & Baby Badger Stencil

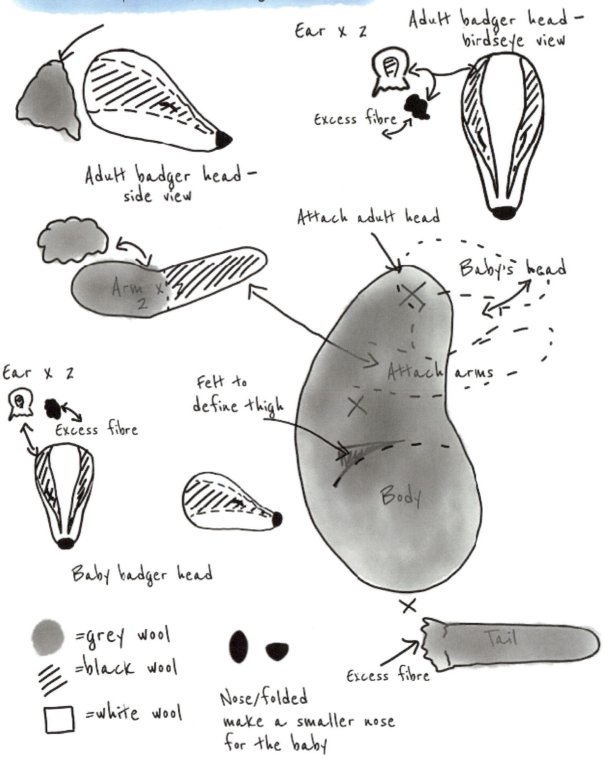

Adult badger head – side view

Ear x 2

Adult badger head – birdseye view

Excess fibre

Attach adult head

Baby's head

Arm x 2

Attach arms

Ear x 2

Excess fibre

Felt to define thigh

Body

Baby badger head

= grey wool

= black wool

= white wool

Nose/folded make a smaller nose for the baby

Excess fibre

Tail

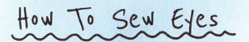

How To Sew Eyes

Tip: Always look from a front view, to ensure the needle is straight before pulling through.

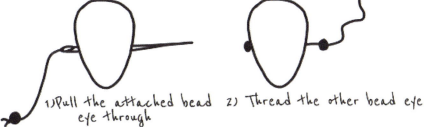

1) Pull the attached bead eye through

2) Thread the other bead eye

3) Go back through the head, exiting at the corner of the other eye

4) Thread the needle back through the hole of the first bead eye

5) Go back through the head again

6) Sign off beneath the head with a blanket stitch

Needle felt a little excess wool fibre over any visible stitches

Coming Soon!

Other books in this series:

Needle Felting - Spring

Needle Felting - Summer

Needle Felting - Autumn

Come back and see us again soon!

Printed in Great Britain
by Amazon